PAST AND PRESENT BATH
a new perspective

BATH, *in common with the world's great cities, lays claim to legendary origins. In the ninth century BC Prince Bladud, son of Ludhudibras and father of Lear, was banished from court owing to his affliction with leprosy. He became a swineherd, and while grazing in the valley of the Avon noted that when his pigs bathed in a certain steaming swamp they emerged cleansed of their sores. Inspired, Bladud immersed himself in the mire and on clambering out found himself muddied but unblemished. Thus restored to health he was welcomed back to court and, in gratitude for his miraculous recovery, founded the city of Bath on the site of the healing springs.* More than a million litres of water pours from these springs every day, water which last saw daylight when it fell on the Mendip hills some ten thousand years ago. Seven thousand years from now, the rain which washed the mud from Bladud's body will pass into the sea. *Past and Present offers a new perspective on an ancient story. It provides a brief overview of Bath's history to give some idea of the forces and personalities which have shaped the town we see today. And it offers a focus on some of the particular aspects and features of Bath which make it unique among towns. Our objective, through words and pictures, is to capture the essence of Bath in all its beauty.*

Published in the United Kingdom
by Past & Present Publications
(a division of Ptarmigan Design
Publishing & Print Limited).

Ptarmigan House
No 9 The Coda Centre
189 Munster Road
London SW6 6AW

Telephone: 0171-381 5600
Facsimile: 0171-381 4012

Editorial	Mark Dawson
Additional Research	The Hon Charles Wilson
Photography	Mark Fiennes
Design and Typesetting	Ptarmigan Design
Front Cover Illustration	Liz Wright
Reproduction	Tower Litho
Print	Graphic Impressions

The author and publishers have made every effort to ensure the accuracy
of the information in this book at the time of going to press. However,
they cannot accept any responsibility for any loss, injury or inconvenience
resulting from the use of information contained in this book.

ISBN 0 9526380 0 2

British Library Cataloguing in Publication Data. A catalogue record for
this book is available from the British Library.

Acknowledgements

Mark Dawson, Mark Fiennes, Gary Parfitt, Liz Wright, Hugh Lefanu, The
Hon Charles Wilson, The Bath Spa Hotel, Lucknam Park, Hunstrete House,
Combe Grove Manor, Homewood Park, The Priory Hotel, Hilton National,
Frances Hotel, The Queensberry Hotel, Stakis Bath, Ston Easton Park, Apsley
House, The General Trading Company, Paxton & Whitfield and Jolly's.

Contents

Before the Romans

THE EARLIEST EVIDENCE of human activity in the Bath area dates from around 5,000 BC. It is no coincidence that small flint blades have been found close to the hot springs: animals are naturally drawn to mineral and salt 'licks', and the concentration of prey in the area of the springs would have become a proven killing ground for hunters. Totally dependent on their immediate environment for survival, these earliest known inhabitants of the area were locked into a limited migratory cycle of winters in the sheltered valleys and summers on higher, more open, territory. ▨ The valley of the *Avon* forms a natural passage between the *Severn* and *Salisbury Plain*, intersecting the *Ridgeway* along its route. Furthermore, the *Jurassic Way*, the great prehistoric route linking the *Wash* to *Dorset*, crossed the Avon where Bath now stands. Doubtless numerous more local routes would also have met at this point, and it is against all the lessons of history that a town of some significance would not have arisen at a place which was the site of so much human interaction. It is often stated as bald fact that Bath would not exist without the springs: while linguistically self-evident, throughout the centuries geography and Bath's situation as a focus of communication have played almost as vital a role in the town's development. ▨ As the forests were cleared and agriculture and the domestication of livestock were introduced into southern Britain, the semi-nomadic way of life gave way to a more settled existence. Pottery and flint remains found on the downs overlooking the Avon valley indicate the upgrowth of a relatively dense population, and the numerous multi-chambered tombs in the vicinity are the marks of a more complex and structured society which provided cohesion within tribally demarcated groups. These tombs are representative of a megalithic tradition which spread northward along the Atlantic seaboard from the Mediterranean basin, a source of inspiration to which the city would twice return in the succeeding centuries. ▨ During the *Bronze Age* the concentration of peoples in Southern England was augmented by an influx of newcomers seeking metals. We now know that during this period of the second and first millennia there was a marked deterioration in the climate, leading to increasing occupation of the valleys as the hilltops became progressively uninhabitable. This climatic shift in turn led to a shift in religious practice, away

■ *HEAD OF A CELTIC GOD*
From the pediment of the Temple of Minerva, probably the work of a gallic craftsman

from the worship of a sky-oriented hill people demonstrated by stone circles and megaliths, and towards woods and water, the natural objects of focus of a valley-dwelling race. The springs at Bath would therefore have been of powerful significance. ▒ Among the local finds from the period of the second millennium BC is a gold 'sun-disc', thought to be of Irish origin, found on Lansdown. It is difficult to avoid association between *Sul*, the local deity representing healing and wisdom, and the sun. We have already referred to a passage of ideas from the Mediterranean: perhaps the Sol of the Romans preceded them to Bath by more than a thousand years, carried from mouth to ear by refugees from Aeneas. ▒ Certainly the name of *Little Solsbury*, the iron age fort situated above *Batheaston* on the eastern approach to Bath, attests to a firm identification of the deity with the location. Initially little more than a cluster of circular wooden huts, later fortified by the addition of a rampart and drystone wall, it was the product of the increasing competition for the use of land brought about by the migration from the moors to the valleys. This conflict also saw the emergence of a mounted warrior class, who were shortly to find themselves confronted by a military force of a power and ruthless efficiency hitherto unimagined in these islands.

■ *LITTLE SOLSBURY*
A view showing the dominant position overlooking Bath of the iron age hilltop fort

Roman Bath

THE SECOND WAVE of Roman invasion under *Claudius* in 43 AD rapidly established control over southern and central England from the *Trent* to the *Severn*. In classic style the invaders set up lines of communication through a network of garrisons linked by roads so efficient that a detachment of legionnaries embarking on the two and half month journey from Rome to Newcastle was expected to reach its destination within twenty-five minutes of its estimated time of arrival. The most important road in the early stages of consolidation was the *Fosse Way*, running from *Poole Harbour* in the south west to *Lincoln* in the east and designed to enable the rapid movement of troops and equipment along the frontier zone . The Romans made use of existing tracks wherever they were of use, and as the site of Bath had for centuries been an important meeting point for routes east to west it was natural that, after striking north from Poole Harbour, the Fosse Way should join and improve the prehistoric *Jurassic Way* at the crossing of the Avon just to the north of where the centre of Bath now stands: indeed there is strong evidence that roads were aligned at this precise point from some distance away. Further roads were later added linking Bath to *London* and to *Sea Mills*, the Roman crossing of the Severn. A permanent garrison would have been established to safeguard the river crossing, although to date no certain evidence of its location has been put forward. (The levelled gravel areas on opposite sides of the river at *Walcot* and *Bathwick* remain the most likely candidates.) It is however clear that the initial presence of the Romans in the area was dictated by military needs rather than the presence of the hot springs. Indeed, as an act of suppression in retaliation for a tribal breach of the frontier in 48-9 AD the occupying forces ran a substantial military road through the immediate vicinity of the springs. From this action it is clear that the springs were perceived by the Romans as of interest only to the natives, that they were held as sacred by the local population, and that in consequence the Romans had hitherto allowed a native sanctuary in the location. It is an incidental measure of their sophistication and habituation to conquest that the religious feelings of the vanquished were treated with such respect. Wherever possible the Romans tried to assimilate the many different phenomena encountered during the growth of the empire, primarily as part of the process of pacification but often in a genuine spirit

of open-mindedness. They would have learned from the local populace of the properties ascribed to the springs, and of *Sul* who presided over their healing powers. As an act of simultaneous appropriation and propitiation the dark northern god was provided with a Mediterranean wife in *Minerva*, the Roman goddess of healing and wisdom, and a temple dedicated to Sulis Minerva was constructed over the springs. In deference to the husband's prior claim the settlement that grew around the garrison and temple as military alertness became increasingly relaxed took the name *Aquae Sulis*, the Waters of Sul. ▨ Aquae Sulis rapidly grew as a centre of recreation. The paving over of the military road through the sacred site confirmed the end of the initial era of repression and signalled the Romans' willingness to establish a peaceful, and of course profitable, relationship with the native population. By the mid-70s a complex of religious and therapeutic buildings constructed from local stone and timber had arisen around the sacred springs. A large altar was placed in the temple forecourt for the sacrifice of animals, with the temple available to all seeking solace or redress from Minerva, whose well-observed martial associations would have established a particularly strong bond with the first military wave of invaders. After an act of petition, visitors would move into the bathing area, specifically designed in its dark and labyrinthine layout to sustain the mystery and miraculous properties of the

■ *HYPOCAUST*

The ingenious Roman system of underfloor heating by circulation of warm air, here used to warm the antechambers of the temple

springs – their natural heat so welcoming to invaders lately arrived from warmer postings to this cold province – until finally reaching the large lead-lined pools for total immersion, either for therapy or relaxation, followed by a contemplative drying-off seated in one of the recesses in the surrounding wall. Temple officials were detailed to curb outbreaks of rowdiness or impropriety, no small task given the barrack-room origins of most of the original clientele.  As the military nature of Aquae Sulis gave way to a more peaceful emphasis, a civilian population grew up both to service the temple and bath complex and to take advantage of the commercial opportunities offered by the town. However, settlement and development of the surrounding area was hampered by Aquae Sulis being the site of several imperial estates, effectively areas of imperial martial law, which the Romans habitually established in key areas of a newly-occupied province to safeguard essential supplies for the occupying forces. Lead, silver, grain, and stone production were under military control from almost the first years of the occupation until well into the third century, and it is only after this period that wealthy citizens were able to construct villas in the area. ▒ This influx of landowners seeking to profit from their agricultural and industrial produce – and it is notable that at this period Britannia was a net exporter of produce to other parts of the empire – meant that Aquae Sulis, though never an official administrative centre, began to take on some of the functions of a market town, serving and being served by a locally-dependent area. There is strong evidence that the suburb which had initially grown up at the road junction in what is now *Walcot* to service the garrison and later the temple and bath, now also became the site of a regular market for locally produced goods. The principal animals raised were sheep and cattle, with arable farming producing cereal, vetch and other pulses, and fruit. Most sites excavated have evidence of ironwork, mainly that of blacksmiths' forges, although there is evidence of smelting: the majority of this work was probably for immediate or local use, but a proportion was almost certainly traded out of the area. ▒ In the second century the imperial forces had felt the need to build a fortified wall around the central precinct of the town, encompassing the temple and baths but excluding the suburbs of Walcot and the garrison (if the garrison was indeed at Walcot/Bathwick). It is not clear what caused this defensive consolidation, although its immediate effect was to condense construction of new dwellings into an increasingly cramped area. However, in the fourth century Britain increasingly became the target for incursions from unconquered northern Europe and Ireland: villas were attacked and burned, and rather

■ THE GREAT BATH
The conduit built by the Romans to carry the overflow from the sacred spring into the River Avon

than rebuild and reoccupy the majority of the owners preferred to take refuge and residence within the walls. Thus increased, the pressure on building land intensified to the extent that materials of the temple were cannibalised: at the same time the dangers of travel and the rising popularity of Christianity would have greatly diminished the numbers of visitors to Aquae Sulis. In 410 a number of British cities applied to the *Emperor Honorius* for protection against the ever-increasing barbarian threat: fully occupied with attempting to preserve the boundaries of a collapsing empire, he advised that no help would be forthcoming. Cut off from its imperial lifeline, this unique example of Romano-British culture disappeared from view in the fifth century AD, whence it would reappear as the inspiration for another cultural miracle only after the passage of thirteen centuries.

■ *THE GREAT BATH*
Rediscovered and excavated
by the Victorians under Major
Davis in 1878

The Dark Ages

THE ROMANS LEFT BRITAIN defenceless as the legions were recalled to defend the heart of the empire against the invading Goths. In the 440s, shortly after *Rome* itself had finally fallen to the barbarians, Saxon raiders invested much of southern and eastern England, the people of the west taking refuge behind Roman walls or reoccupying the hilltop forts left deserted during the centuries of Roman peace. From this miasma of legend and half-history great leaders emerged, including the warrior king *Arthur* who led the defence of the western realm against the West Saxons. This rearguard struggle culminated in a victory in the early fifth century on *Mons Badonicus* (Mount Badon), an unknown site for which the most likely location is the hills overlooking Bath — *Badon* being one of the names later bestowed on the town. However, this reverse only temporarily halted Saxon expansion, and the decisive conflict of the *Battle of Dyrham* in 577 finally handed to the invaders the towns of *Gloucester*, *Cirencester*, and *Bath*, three native 'kings' being slain in the battle. The all-important routes on which it stood established Bath as an important foothold for the West Saxon leader *Caewlin*: it also brought him into contact with the Saxon kingdom of *Mercia* to the north. ▨ A period of conflict between the two forces was eventually resolved in 628 when the Mercians defeated the West Saxons at Cirencester, forcing the latter to retreat to south of the Avon. The *West Wansdyke* earthwork was constructed to mark the political boundary between Mercia and the new kingdom of *Wessex*, and Bath became the principal place of passage between the two kingdoms, with a consequent resurgence of civic importance. In 676 *Osric*, deputy king of Mercia, granted land to the *Abbess Berta* (or Bertana) for the construction of a nunnery of holy virgins in the city of *'Hat Bathu'*. Although the precise location of the foundation is unknown, it would certainly have stood within the old walls and have benefited during construction from the ready supply of materials from the crumbling buildings left by the Romans. ▨ For one of the most concrete consequences of the victory of the Saxons was the rapid deterioration of the edifice of *Aquae Sulis*. The complex of baths rapidly fell into disrepair, with plumbing and conduits becoming choked with mud and slime. Over the years the marsh reclaimed areas of the town which had been hard won by the Roman genius for works of civil engineering, and waterfowl made their nests in the temple of *Minerva*. To the comparatively uncouth invaders the remains of the city were a source of wonder, and after the nunnery had been transformed into a monastery dedicated to *St Peter* some time in the eighth century a monk wrote *'The Ruin'*, a poem that survives only in fragments but which contains a powerful sense of the awe which the remains, "fortifications raised by giants", inspired in its new inhabitants. ▦ During the ninth century a new threat arose from the north, and it was during the reign of *Alfred the Great*, king of Wessex from 871 to 899, that the fortifications of Bath were strengthened against possible Danish attack. At some time immediately prior to this period Bath had passed back from Mercia to Wessex, and Bath began to take up a position as a town of far more than local significance. The growing fame of its monastery, coupled with a strategic economic position as the hub of a network of trade routes, encouraged Bath's growth as a market town of importance. Alfred's successor, *Edward the Elder*, reinforced the defences of Wessex, and it may have been during his reign that a mint was established for the issue of silver coins. Under *Athelstan* a leper's hospital was founded in the city, and the regularisation of the street plan bespeaks the growing prosperity enjoyed by a secure population under strong royal patronage. Final confirmation of the town's pre-eminence arrived with its selection as the natural location for the coronation of *Edgar* who, having become ruler of *Mercia* and *Northumbria* two years previously, was the first to be crowned as king of all England. ▦ However, the period of optimism introduced by the coronation was short-lived. Edgar died suddenly after two years with no natural successor, and once again the northern menace was looming. It is not known for certain whether any Norse attempt was made on the city: fragments of a Viking sword have been found in the excavated protective ditch, but this was probably the relic of an isolated and relatively frivolous expedition, and the non-navigability of the *Avon* from the *Severn* was more than likely of greater protective benefit. The Vikings may have been unwilling to commit large land forces in a protracted attempt on a heavily fortified town: more to the point, they may not have felt the need, for during the reign of *Aethelred II* (978-1016) silver coins destined for hoards in Scandinavia were minted in Bath in ever-increasing abundance to supply the *Danegeld*. To little avail: in 1013 *Sweyn of Denmark* became overlord of the west, according to some reports having attacked and taken prisoners in Bath, and in 1016 *Cnut* was unopposed in claiming the throne of united England, establishing a line which would stand for only half a century before the southern colonists of the Norsemen became the last race to succeed in invading this island.

The Middle Ages

IT WOULD APPEAR from *Chaucer's* text that it was important that it was from Bath that the wife came on her pilgrimage to Canterbury (the rhyme 'that was scathe' merely means 'which was a pity') so what associations would his readers in the late fourteenth century have been led to make by this pinpointing of her provenance? ☷ As with the first Roman invasion, so immediately after the *Norman Conquest* in 1066 little immediate effect was felt in Bath. The *Domesday* Survey of 1086 recorded a local economy dominated by the church, which held one third of the land within the city and seventeen villages in the immediate vicinity, which with private landholdings supplied the wool which dominated local trade. The majority of the remaining land was held by the King. The mint changed its stamps and was to continue to produce coins bearing the heads of Norman kings until well into the twelfth century. However, this quiet existence received an abrupt interruption in 1087 when *William I* died, leaving his kingdom divided between his sons *Robert of Mowbray*, who held Normandy, and *William Rufus*, who was granted the new English lands. Mowbray and his supporters rebelled in an attempt to reunite the two realms, ravaging Bath and its surrounding area from their base in *Bristol*. The rebellion finally suppressed, *Rufus* rewarded a powerful supporter by installing *John de Villula Bishop of Tours*, in the newly vacant seat of *Bishop of Wells* Thus was introduced the first of the many personalities whose individual drive and vision were to shape the Bath we see today. ☷ John of Tours first step was to remove his seat from Wells to Bath, in line with the current practice of siting cathedra in larger communities. Possibly because the local economy had been so devastated by Mowbray as to be of little worth, Rufus shortly afterwards handed over to John of Tours the rest of the town, and the bishop eagerly seized this unique opportunity to rebuild Bath according to his personal plan. Ignoring the late Saxon layout of the town, John began a vast new cathedral in a new religious precinct which included not only the churches of *St Mary de Stalles* and *St James*, probably built during the later Saxon period in the tenth century, but what is now known as the *King's Spring* ☷ John of Tours was the first man of power since the Romans to see the hot springs as a source of anything but

"A good wif was ther of biside Bathe, But she was somdel deef, and that was scathe."

superstitious awe. An outstanding physician as well as a powerful church dignitary, John was particularly interested in the medicinal properties claimed for the springs. He reopened the bath for bathing purposes, building individual stone seats into the walls of the surviving rectangular building left by the Romans, naming the complex the *King's Bath* after *Henry I*, the second of his royal patrons. During the reconstruction of the baths *Geoffrey of Monmouth*, citing an unnamed earlier source, first recorded the legend of *Bladud*, creating a therapeutic continuum and useful public relations for the new enterprise. ▦ John of Tours died in 1122, to be followed by a number of equally

■ *HOSPITAL OF ST JOHN
Founded in 1174 by Bishop
Reginald Fitzjocelyn to enable
the poor and sick to take the
waters*

enthusiastic successors. *Robert of Lewes* continued with work on the cathedral and bath, which seems to have been of immediate and more than local interest. In 1138 it was reported in the anonymous *Gesta Stephani*, written under the direction of bishop Robert, that "sick persons from all over England resort thither to bathe in these healing waters, and the fit also". The smaller springs outside the monastery grounds – the *Hot* and *Cross Baths* – were also developed around this time under the Bishop's rule, with the healing motif established by John maintained by the foundation in 1174 of the *Hospital of St John the Baptist*[2] under bishop *Reginald Fitzjocelyn*. ✠ In the seventy five years between the elevation of John of Tours and the death of Robert of Lewes in 1166, Bath had witnessed the creation of one of the largest churches in England, ancillary buildings – bishop's residence, chapter house, cloister, infirmary, refectory – appropriate to that status, and the rejuvenation of Bath as a national centre of healing pilgrimage. However, this achievement rested on the energy, power, and interest of two visionary bishops, and the decline of the seat proved almost as rapid. In 1245 the Pope decreed that Bath should share its status with Wells, the see being thereafter known as Bath and Wells. Bishops increasingly preferred to perform their duties in the more modern palace at Wells, built in the late twelfth century, and in 1328 the letting to the prior of the palace at Bath proved final confirmation of the bishop's lack of interest in the town. Lacking the motivation and inspiration of a bishop on site, morale among the monks fell, as allegedly did moral standards, and as revenues fell the fabric of the buildings fell into disrepair. In 1348 a visitation of the *Black Death* reduced the numbers of the monks from forty to less than twenty, and the story of Bath as a seat of religious authority was effectively over. ✠ However, the confidence and energy originally invested by John of Tours in the town, supported by the booming wool trade, ensured a solid foundation for the secular community. During the twelfth century economic activity escalated, and some shrewd timing by the elders of the guilds – petitioning for a royal charter from *Richard I*, desperate to raise funds, four days before the king set forth on the *Third Crusade* – brought freedom from royal tolls on the movement of goods. As economic activity increased, so naturally did the spread of the town. Within the walls, which had been strengthened by *King Stephen* in 1138 but which were now once again more a quarry than a defence, the monastery and its outbuildings took up all otherwise unoccupied land, and the twelfth century saw the beginnings of the spread of the town along the roads outside the South and North gates, with the latter area considerably more

favoured than the marshy and flood-prone southern plots. And as the town grew, so the walls took on a more symbolic significance, marking out the territory within which the privileges of the royal charter obtained, and further bonding a sense of community within those so privileged. ▓ The interdependence between the town and its hinterland came to reside in the wool trade, the mainstay of the local economy. All the essentials for a thriving trade were found in a single area, from the raw material grazing in abundance on the surrounding downs to the water flowing in the valleys, to the centuries-old network of roads for the export of finished produce and the import of other requirements and, equally important, news and new ideas; all served by the fullers, spinners, weavers, dyers, and tailors based in the town. ▓ This then is what Bath would have meant to *Chaucer*'s readers: a small town grown prosperous through a single nationally-renowned trade, clothmaking, which (with her five late husbands) was the principal source of the Wife of Bath's wealth, and the produce of which Chaucer with patriotic fervour avers exceeded in quality the now more famous stuffs produced in Ypres and Ghent.

Civic Pride and Civil War

THE DISSOLUTION of the monasteries, elsewhere so disruptive to the lives of communities which depended on the maintenance of a religious economic centre, had a somewhat different effect in Bath. In many ways the *Monastery of St Peter* had become an irrelevance to the life of the town, and when *Bishop Oliver King* visited Bath in 1499 he found a church beyond repair attended by demoralised servants. The presiding prior died shortly after Bishop King's visit, and it was to the new prior, *William Birde*, that King entrusted the task of restoring the status of the religious community by rebuilding the cathedral, following a dream wherein a ladder was seen with angels ascending and descending, and a voice cried "Let an olive establish the crown and a king restore the church". The remains of the Norman cathedral were to be pulled down, and a smaller edifice erected in its place. Hired for the task were *William* and *Robert Vertue*, royal masons and prime exponents of the late mediaeval art of fan vaulting, who promised King the finest chancel vault in Western Europe. Before they could realise this promise, other constraints led to *Henry VIII* becoming head of the Church of England, and to the commissioning of a nationwide survey into the moral and, more importantly, material conditions of the ecclesiastical infrastructure. Reports from Bath echoed and embellished the long decay that had afflicted the monastery since the late twelfth century, and – reading the writing on the wall – the prior, *William Holloway*, disposed of the remaining church properties to local landowners. In 1539 the new Abbey was handed over to the Crown, leaving Bath without a monastery for the first time in eight and a half centuries. The almost brand new Abbey, however, was also in a state of some decrepitude. Realising the lack of revenue likely to accrue from his new acquisition, party due to the machinations of Holloway and partly to the fact that the cloth industry was at that time going through one of its temporary and periodic declines leading to the collapse of property values and the neglect of houses within the city, Henry offered the Abbey to the town for a mere 500 marks. Unable or unwilling to pay even this paltry price the offer was declined, and for several more years the church stood as a source of lead and glass for local enterprises before passing through various hands into the control of the Corporation in 1572. Many local citizens had benefited considerably by the dispersal of church property as it passed from hand

to hand, with a resultant increase in the power of the civic authorities. These were now responsible both for the upkeep of the Abbey and for the spiritual judgements previously under its sway, but showed as little enthusiasm for either as the monks had. ▦ What forced the Corporation to exert themselves in attending to at least the material needs of the Abbey was the steady influx of visitors to the baths, which in turn heralded the transformation of Bath's economic dependence from an industrial centre based on wool to what we would now call a service economy. The Elizabethan *Poor Law Acts* named the Baths of Bath and Buxton as places to which the sick poor might legitimately have free access, partly to prevent foreign travel and consequent exposure to seditious Catholic dogma, and because such royal advertisement naturally attracted more wealthy guests. In 1562, the Dean of Wells (*Dr William Turner*), published his *Treatise on the Bath Waters* which, while endorsing the medicinal claims of the waters, criticised the shoddy and inadequate facilities available to visitors. In 1574 the Queen herself paid a visit, prompting a new wave of improvements and the beginning of Bath's social exclusivity. As an aid to decorum the *Queen's Bath* was built for women alongside the *King's Bath*, and no doubt to siphon off some of the less sightly the *Leper' Bath* was constructed next to the *Hot Bath*: finally, the *Horse Bath* was built outside the city walls. Fashionable court clientele were now coming to Bath

■ SARACEN'S HEAD
In Broad Street, original starting point of the 'Exeter Diligence' and one of the many hostelries which competed for wealthy visitors

in increasing numbers, while the numbers of poor and diseased people entering the town had been limited by Parliamentary statute, and to capitalise on the town's fast-growing reputation wealthy townspeople further invested their acquisitions of old priory land by building lodging houses for visitors. ▓ During all this time the traditional economic base of undyed broadcloth production continued, subject as ever to the vagaries of an unstable international market. Much of the cloth produced went, via London wholesalers and a well-established international market, to the Low Countries and the German principalities for finishing and retail. The outbreak of the *Thirty Years' War* in 1618 disastrously disrupted the crucial continental market: by 1622, distress among Bath's clothworkers was widespread, and although a change of focus seems to be implied by the weekly cloth market which began in an echo of *Aquae Sulis* at this time in *Walcot*, this would have been of far less value as a source of income than the thriving international trade it sought to replace. ▓ The hot springs, however, continued to provide a regular supply of business to lodging-house keepers, medical practitioners, bath personnel, and the army of tradesmen required to service the blossoming trade based on extensive visits to the town. Like their forebears the Romans the Corporation appointed attendants to assist bathers and ensure proper order, and rules were laid down for the refilling of the baths and for the supply of cold water for the public drinking fountains. Such measures, as well as the continuance of the propaganda begun by *Geoffrey of Monmouth* and continued by medical writers in the early seventeenth century, ensured that Bath more than held its own in competition with *Buxton* and *Tunbridge Wells* for wealthy patrons. The biggest fish were of course royalty, and although *Elizabeth* never made her promised return trip *Anne of Denmark*, queen of *James I*, came twice in 1613 and again in 1615. Assiduously courted by the *Mayor* and Corporation, little of the revenues accruing from such visits went to the town, instead being destined for the already stretched pockets of those prominent citizens providing lodgings, food, drink, and medical services. ▓ The great schism of the mid-seventeenth century placed Bath in a profound dilemma. *The West Country*, more than most provincial regions, has always been a focus of non-conformist dissent. During the 1630's episcopal attempts to enforce the *Laudian* liturgy and silence protestant preachers, combined with *Charles I's* suppression of Parliament and repeated demands for ship money, polarised the country. *Somerset*, and with it Bath, came down on the side of Parliament. It is hard to determine how much the Corporation's decision was based on strongly held conviction, and how much on a pragmatic desire to remain in step with its surrounding county. Certainly there was considerable support for the Royalist cause from a group headed by *Henry Chapman*, a landowner with sizeable investments in lodging-houses, and a significant minority remained uncommitted. And equally certainly Bath had to a great degree identified its prosperity with precisely those people against whom the Parliamentary cause was most rigorously opposed. ▨ In 1643 the town fell to the Royalists under *Sir Ralph Hopton*, and for two years

■ *THE CROSS BATH*
The most fashionable bath of the Restoration era, given a new exterior by John Wood in the eighteenth century

was systematically barricaded and fortified as a Royalist stronghold. Farcically, after so much effort having drained the reserves of townspeople and Corporation, rejoiced in only by Chapman and his fellows, the town exchanged hands without a struggle when a scouting party sent by *Fairfax* in 1645 gained entry at the *South Gate* and the Royalist Governor, believing himself surrounded by an army, surrendered the town and a considerable arsenal without a struggle. ▨ Bath remained under Parliamentary control for the following fifteen years. Chapman was initially retained on the city council, but in 1647 that conciliatory body finally felt it necessary to expel this thorn in their side and six of his colleagues: the following April Chapman defied all authority by having the abolished prayer book read openly in *St James'* church, and by organising bull-baitings. During the period of the Commonwealth prominent visitors continued to avail themselves of the healing waters, including in 1658 *Richard Cromwell*, the new Lord Protector, but a city built on catering to fashionable guests was becoming as weary as the rest of the country with the prevailing austerity, and was looking forward with eagerness to the restoration of a monarchy to serve.

Restoration and Speculation

IN ORDER TO STAY AHEAD of the competition, Bath had to court favour and secure patronage at the highest level. Thus despite having settled on the Parliamentary side at the outbreak of civil war, it was the first town to proclaim *Charles II* and deliver a loyal address, and effective reward was granted when the King and Queen bathed in the now fashionable *Cross Bath* in 1663. The period saw Bath deliberately promoted as a health resort and loyal city, including the first appearance of an advertisement in a London newspaper. At the same time the cloth industry was in a decline that would this time be permanent, to the extent that by the 1680's it had become plain to *Thomas Dingley* that Bath's transformation from a manufacturing to a service economy was complete, and that Bathonians "chiefly get their bread by... the Baths". To complement this new focus of commercial energy, the old patchwork of ancient and decrepit dwellings within the walls was being superseded by new buildings: the bathing establishments had been improved, and other amenities included a coffee house, a bowling green, and landscaped walks laid out to the east of the *Abbey*, while sedan chairs for hire allowed the gentry to circulate easily among these attractions. ▓ Having experienced its own restoration to favour, the town found itself at the centre of the political upheavals attendant on the succession of the Catholic *James II*. After some agonising it came down on the side of the monarch against the *Duke of Monmouth's* protestant insurgents, leading to the shutting of the city gates to Monmouth's army and the brutal execution in the town of four of the rebels after the battle of *Sedgemoor*. This allegiance was not universally appreciated, and was further compounded by the part it played in the King's downfall. After bathing in the waters *Mary*, his queen, conceived, and while the town eagerly tried to capitalise on this triumph for the properties of the hot springs, many others in the country felt that a perpetuation of a Catholic dynasty was beyond endurance. *William of Orange* was invited to invade, and within months James had fled. ▓ Bath had comprehensively backed and abetted the loser, and set about trying to make amends and curry favour with the new orthodoxy. Although for some time tainted with the suspicion of Jocobitism – when *Princess Anne*, thought to desire James' reinstatement, visited in 1692 a government informer reported on her contacts – such royal visits, however troublesome, further supported the therapeutic claims of the waters. The

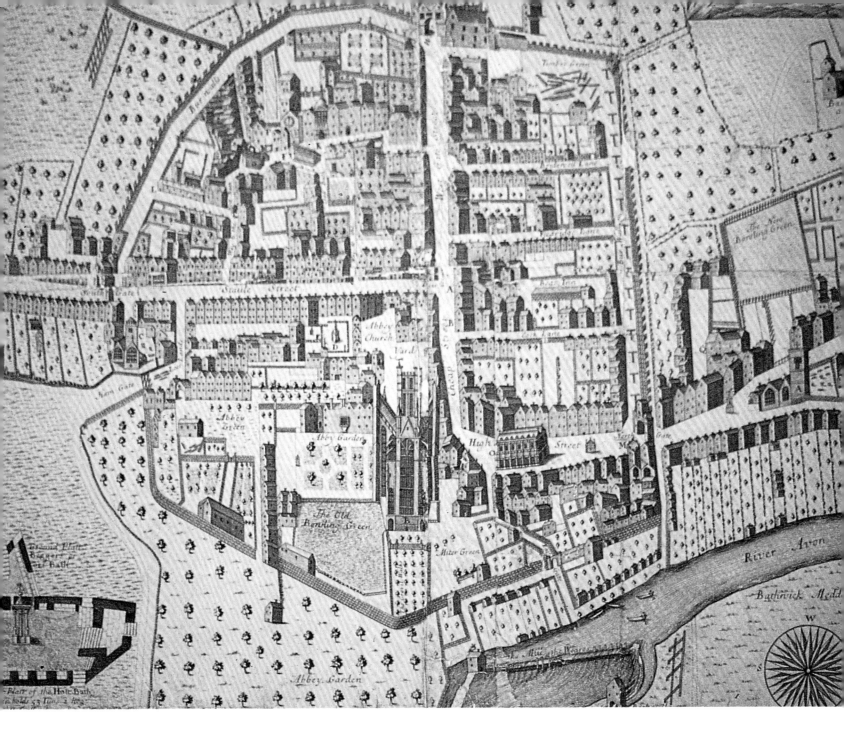

visits of Queen Anne in 1702 and 1703 confirmed Bath's pre-eminent status, and the Corporation took note of its obligations to consolidate this position in the face of competition from other spa towns by erecting a gracious *Pump Room* in 1706 and by obtaining an Act of Parliament in 1708 to improve street amenities. 🔳 However, it is no exaggeration to state that Bath would not exist in its current form without speculation, and Bath's popularity with fashionable society might have faded had it not been for the convergence of one of the small band of extraordinary individuals with which its history has been blessed and the passion which had obsessed the gentry since the restoration: gambling. In the early years of the eighteenth century Bath was a byword for 'deep play', whereby vast sums would change hands on the turn of a card, and card-sharps, prostitutes and their pimps, and the whole ragged band naturally

■ *PLAN OF BATH*
Drawn in 1692-94 by
Thomas Gilmore, 'Teacher of
the Mathematicks' in the City
of Bristol. It shows the late
mediaeval town which made
way for modern Bath

drawn to a scene of such swiftly-moving currency was firmly in place around the rich men's tables. Gamblers lower down the social scale were amply catered for by cockfights, billiards, raffling shops, and the newly-established race course on *Claverton Down*. ▦ *Richard "Beau" Nash* (so nicknamed due to the beauty of his manners rather than any pulchritude of feature, as contemporary records and portraits forcefully confirm) was an adventurer and professional gambler who had arrived in Bath in 1704, attracted by the lively action at the tables. Despite his comparative lack of success in his previous careers as a soldier and lawyer, Nash was a man of highly-developed social perceptions and immediately realised that if the resort was to remain in fashion it would need to set, rather than merely follow, the standards for polite society. His elevation in 1705 to the post of *Master of Ceremonies* – and it speaks for Bath's status as an acknowledged "Valley of Pleasure" that such a post existed, and to the hitherto lack of status accorded the post that Nash was so swiftly able to secure it – when the previous incumbent gave him the platform from which to express his views, and over the course of a fifty year career subsidised by cards and dice Nash became the social linchpin of Bath and the arbiter of manners throughout a much wider orbit. In the process, Bath's position as the centre of the world of fashion, elegance, and mannered society was assured for generations. ▦ Due to his position and growing influence, Nash was able to act as a medium between the Corporation, tradesman at heart anxious only for a stable field of operations, and the wildly fluctuating cast of visitors with their equally fluctuating fortunes. Ultimately the success of Nash in inhibiting the wilder elements and raising the expectations of society counted against his greatest passion: in 1738 and 1739 the two assembly rooms on which he was financially dependent lost money, and one was heavily fined for shady operations. As a result several of most popular games were banned, and neither Nash nor the tables recovered from this blow. By 1750 serious gambling had been driven underground, and Nash spent his declining years with his mistress *Juliana Popjoy* (a lady of somewhat tarnished reputation: on being accused of 'whoremongering', Nash famously replied "a man can no more be accused of being a whoremonger for having one whore in the house, than a cheesemonger for having one cheese") an impoverished but still generally respected figure in the town. His influence had been due to his official position in the town, but his sympathies were always with the gamesters, and it was gamblers of another sort who were to effect as profound a change on the physical appearance of the city as Nash had achieved in its social aspect.

Seizing the Day

I T WAS THE SECOND manifestation of the new passion for speculation, combined with Bath's centuries-old importance as a focus for communications, that enabled the transformation from a late mediaeval hotch-potch to the harmonious appearance with which Bath now presents itself. And true to form, also to the fore were the last two of the triumvirate who can justly lay claim to having shaped the Bath we see today. ▨ *Ralph Allen* arrived in Bath as assistant to the post-mistress in 1710, succeeding her two years later to become the youngest postmaster in the country. It is often suggested, without firm supportive evidence, that it was his no doubt ex officio habit of opening the mails which enabled him in 1715 to win the patronage of *General Wade* by exposing a Jacobite plot in the South West. Whatever the reason, as a result he was awarded lucrative contracts running the cross-country mails, which rapidly made him a personal fortune. This fortune enabled him to subsidise the opening of the *Avon* to navigation, which in turn made profitable the purchase and development of the limestone quarries on *Combe Down*, providing him with the wherewithal to supply the raw materials for the inspirational, and in origin undoubtedly eccentric, plans of the third founding father of modern Bath, *John Wood*. ▨ Wood was an architect who had been born in Bath but had spent much of his early career in Yorkshire and London. Returning to his native city in 1727, he was fired by an extraordinary vision of recreating Bath along the lines of its first civic inspiration, classical *Rome*. Fired by his fervour for the glories of antiquity, Wood proposed to the Corporation a complete remodelling of the city with a *Forum*, a *Circus Maximus*, and other buildings modelled on ancient Rome. Perhaps unsurpris-ingly the Corporation received these proposals with a marked lack of enthusiasm, nor were they in a financial to position to support such an undertaking. ▨ What lay ahead demonstrated that Wood was man not only of architectural but also of financial vision. In 1700 all the land in or around Bath was corporately or privately owned, but difficult to develop for profit. In accordance with the local West Country practice, property was leased in small pockets and a leased property could not revert to its owner until all three lives on the lease were extinguished, while during the period of the lease the landowner would only receive a meagre rent, waiting on the lease renewal or transfer

■ *THE KENNET & AVON CANAL*
Ralph Allen was treasurer of the company which opened the canal for navigation

fees for larger revenues. Thus the consolidation of sufficient pockets of property into a plot suitable for development, and therefore attracting larger rents, could be an extremely lengthy process. In 1640 the 329 acres of the *Walcot Lordship* were worth £10 a year: by 1790 they had become among the most valuable properties in the country, purely as a result of the radical new methods of raising and spreading the costs of development introduced by Wood. ▨ Wood's first residential development, *Chandos Buildings*, had been financed by a single wealthy individual. For *Queen's Square*, his next grandiose project, Wood mobilised a hitherto untapped source of investment capital. One *Robert Gay* held an unleased piece of land just to the north west of the city: for this site Wood proposed an elegant square of private dwellings, devised as a single development with as its focus a mock palace on the northern side. Over the space of six years Gay released the required land in twelve plots, for a total annual rent of £137 per annum. Wood then granted building leases for each house to individual builders, who undertook to complete their side of the contract within a given period in return for paying only a token rent while construction was in progress. The builder built the property to Wood's specification, financed by a mortgage secured by the building lease, and once the shell was completed advertised for a buyer: with the clamour for accommodation in Bath at this period very few were unsuccessful. The buyer paid the builder a lump sum for the shell of the house, and paid the developer an annual rent. From Queen's Square these rents provided Wood with annual income of £305, a profit of £168 after paying the rent due to Gay. Provided the chain of credit held good everyone involved from Gay to the builder therefore earned a safe return on his investment at a low individual risk. ▓ These building ventures were speculative in that the builder gambled on being able to find a buyer and for the market to be sufficiently favourable to enable a profit over and above the costs of construction. In truth, such was the clamour for accommodation in Bath from seasonal visitors and from a burgeoning residential population that the odds on making money were firmly in favour of the speculator. As many as five thousand visitors arrived at the end of each summer, with many of their number staying for the duration of the winter, and as long as the tradespeople of Bath could enjoy profitable business between September and May they were happy to accept three fallow months before the new season began. ▓ The profitable completion of Queen's Square inspired confidence in speculators to finance Wood's next project, the Parades, a scaled-down version of his original plan for a Forum. Catering to the fashion for promenading, it also opened up *Spring Garden* on the opposite bank of the Avon. Further developments saw Wood advancing by the

■ *COMBE GROVE MANOR HOTEL & COUNTRY CLUB*
A classic 18th century country house hotel just outside Bath. Each of the nine bedrooms within the Manor House has been individually designed, a further 31 tastefully decorated rooms are available in the adjacent Garden Lodge

construction of *Gay Street* up the hill from Queen's Square towards what was to become his most impressive project, and the most powerful monument to his never-realised plan for the recreation of Rome on the Avon: the *Circus*. ▓ The Circus is an expression of a tri-unity which increasingly obsessed Wood. Designed to echo the *Colosseum*, the three great crescents of the Circus, intersticed with their three exit roads, featured columns of all three Greek orders of architecture. The parapets were adorned with acorns in reference to the *Bladud* myth in which Wood fervently believed, establishing a confluence of three traditions of antiquity into which Wood wished to re-establish his home town. The first two crescents were rapidly completed, but an untimely drying up of credit delayed the completion of the project until 1766: however, the visionary whose extraordinary designs, both architectural and financial, had done so much to assist the creation of a new town, had died twelve years before, leaving his son *John* to oversee the final realisation of his most cherished dream.

Beauty Through Harmony

THE OVERRIDING first impression of any visitor to Bath is of architectural harmony, to the extent that the town seems almost to have been designed according to a single plan. The first and most obvious explanation for this is simply that the majority of what we now see was built over what, in terms of the development of a town of Bath's size, was an astonishingly short period. Moreover a single architectural style exercised an overwhelming dominance over the era. This derived from the teachings of the Venetian *Andrea Palladio*, and emphasised the overriding importance of symmetry and harmony based on classical models. The first great builder of Bath, the elder *John Wood*, was as firm an adherent of the *Palladian* style as his contemporaries, perhaps especially so owing to his peculiar, almost mystic, attachment to the resonances of history. ▨ In order to satisfy the terms of his contract each individual builder was legally obliged to construct the façade of his building according to the designs of the architect, which were generally drawn on the reverse of the lease, and it was part of the architect's function to ensure that builders did not diverge from the agreed design. Where an architect was not the presiding genius behind a scheme, many Georgian buildings were designed by 'master builders'. These master builders were prosperous, practical men who relied not on inspiration and grand schemes but on their long experience. And as these builders were also speculators, their overriding concern was to find a buyer for the property and thereby recover and make a profit on the expense of building it. In these circumstances, to have designed a building against the prevailing orthodoxy would have been commercially foolhardy: what was required for developers and builders alike were houses that conformed to the prevailing fashion for order and symmetry, and which were sufficiently modern in appearance to attract a buyer. In this the builders were greatly aided by the many pattern books published throughout the eighteenth century, from which a builder could select designs for each feature of the house under construction. The speculative nature of the exercise further tended towards conformity, since in a profit-based enterprise the best method is the shortest between

■ *GAY STREET*

Named after the surgeon who owned the land on which it and Queen's Square now stand

two points and any attempt at architectural innovation would thus have represented a waste of valuable resources of time and energy. In the building boom which overtook Bath in the mid eighteenth century, the elder Wood had created the benchmark for profitable design in *Queen's Square*. Even in the high period of speculation no-one was prepared to gamble against the precedent established by Wood. ▓ Finally, *Ralph Allen's* entrepreneurial skills were to have a enduring legacy in the prevailing beauty of the honey-coloured soft limestone used throughout the town. The stone had been quarried since Roman times, but it was Allen who, by buying up land for quarries and exploiting new technology – most notably the ingenious railway designed for him by *John Padmore* – ensured that it could be available to builders in sufficient quantities and at a sufficiently low price to make it viable as a building material, although it was still too expensive to be used as anything other than a thin facing over rougher materials. When it is remembered that a different builder would often be responsible for the masonry of each house in a row of properties, the smoothness and continuity of the façades is truly remarkable. ▓ However, the requirement of the builder to conform, whether contractual or commercial, stopped at the façade. The builder was under no constraints regarding the rear of the building, nor was he generally concerned with anything more than the structure of the property. The occupier would buy the completed shell of the house, and in most cases contracted separately with plasterers, carpenters and decorators to finish the interior. Thus while Bath exhibits an extraordinary homogeneity of exterior appearances, no two interiors are alike. One of the few opportunities open to the owner to demonstrate his own preference and taste was in selecting the doorcase, albeit a selection made from the builder's pattern book: the base price of the property included the basic doorcase, but at additional cost the occupant could parade his discernment, or perhaps merely his wealth, by selecting from a range of more ostentatious entrances. ▓ As *Smollett* implied, two very different priorities were often at odds in the construction of Georgian Bath. The developer was interested in a trouble-free tenancy and a regular annual rent over the full 99 years of the lease, whereas the builder was interested merely in ensuring a profit over the cost of construction, and had little or no interest in which of the property or the lease lasted the longest. It is no small tribute to the vigilance of the surveyors employed by architects to oversee construction, and also to the prevailing high standards of construction, that so much of Georgian Bath still stands in all its elegant glory.

■ *THE GEORGIAN DOORCASE*
One of the few ways in which the buyer of a property could demonstrate superior taste to his neighbour

"...the rage for building has laid hold on such a number of adventurers that one sees new houses starting up... in every corner of Bath; contriv'd without judgement, executed without solidity... built so slight... that I should never sleep quietly in one of them". TOBIAS SMOLLETT
Humphrey Clinker (1871)

The High Georgian Era

BEAU NASH died in 1761, laid low financially by reverses on the tables and embittered by what he saw as the persecution of his business operations, but retaining to the end his benign dictatorship over the polite society of Bath. The elegance and vigour he had brought to the position of Master of Ceremonies over more than half a century proved impossible to replace. After eight years and two further incumbents there ensued a fierce contest for the post which culminated in open brawling ended only by the third reading of the Riot Act by the mayor. Though farcical in hindsight, and the cause of much satire at the time, the descent of the powdered gentility into a riotous mob at least illustrates the importance brought to a position the outsider Nash had so easily acquired. ▧ Those now voting for the Master of Ceremonies were in many cases a new breed to Bath, being well-off upper middle class residents rather than temporary visitors, the result of a self-perpetuating spiral of successful investment in residential development increasing the social éclat of Bath, leading to increased demand, which in turn led to further development. The period 1765 to 1775 saw the appearance of a substantial upper town spreading north and into the hills around *Walcot*, with *Wood the younger's Upper Assembly Rooms* as the most direct challenge to the authority of the established lower town. The old centre also expanded across *Kingsmead*, while *Pulteney Bridge* opened the way for development to the East across the river. Within the space of several decades Bath was transformed from a country town delineated by its mediaeval limits into one of the largest towns in England. ▧ This extraordinary growth brought its own social problems. Unskilled labourers were drawn to a site of such activity in vast numbers, most settling in the slum areas at the southern end of the town. Bath had always had a lively underclass, but to its traditional low-grade circus of prostitutes, pimps, small-stake gamblers and conmen was added the new threat of political unrest. In 1770 a mob responded to the Gordon riots in London by burning down the just-opened Catholic chapel, and throughout the next thirty years – and especially at the height of the French revolution – reformist and radical groups were seen as a constant menace to the presentation of Bath as a centre of decorum. ▧ However, by now the town was advancing under its own momentum. No longer dependent on royal patronage – no reigning *Hanoverian* ever

■ *GRAVEL WALK*
Between Royal Crescent and Queen's Parade, and where Captain Wentworth and Anne Elliott famously declared their love in 'Persuasion'

■ THE ASSEMBLY ROOMS
*The Upper Rooms rapidly
eclipsed their older rivals as the
most fashionable in town: the
basement now houses the famous
Museum of Costume*

visited Bath – visitors arrived in ever-increasing numbers. Despite its poverty-stricken
underclass and vulnerability to the fluctuating confidence of capital, the image of the
Bath of this era is that so memorably painted by *Jane Austen* – at once a retreat from
the real world and a feverish forum for business of all kinds, a maze of romantic and
pecuniary intrigue, a stage for conspicuous consumption and egregious ostentation
– which is perhaps our most vivid association with the town. A well-defined social
round was established: bathing, followed by assembly in the *Pump Room* for
conversation while taking the recommended dose of three glasses of water; coffee
(separate coffee houses were frequented by the sexes), would precede breakfast. The
day was then left free for a round of social visits or promenading with acquaintances,
in preparation for an evening at one of the many concerts, parties, or formal balls
which formed an integral and continual part of the Bath season. ❖ As Austen

■ APSLEY HOUSE HOTEL
*Standing amid delightful gardens,
this elegant Georgian hotel occupies
a house reputedly built for the Duke
of Wellington just one mile from the
centre of Bath.*

■ *THE PUMP ROOM*

The fashionable location in which to congregate for the morning exchange of opinion and intrigue after the regulation intake of spa water

confirms with her customary elegance, in comparison with London, Bath was inescapably provincial, and in this reduction of scale and scope lay much of its charm. Between his election to the post of Master of Ceremonies in 1704 and his death in 1761 Nash had codified and established the rules of etiquette which became the benchmark for polite society throughout England, and his achievement was only possible owing to the comparatively small scale of the empire over which he held sway. The measure of his success is best left to Bath's ironic chronicler:

'Bath, compared with London, has little variety, and so every body finds out each year. "For six weeks, I allow Bath is pleasant enough; but beyond that it is the most tiresome place in the world". You would be told so by people of all descriptions, who come regularly each winter, lengthen their six weeks into ten or twelve, and go away at last because they can afford to stay no longer.'

JANE AUSTEN
Northanger Abbey

The Coming of the Railway

THE ARRIVAL IN BATH of *Brunel's Great Western Railway*, by which it was connected to *Bristol* in 1840 and to *London* in 1841, brought with it a resurgence of civic hopes which had become depressed in the years immediately after 1830. Many causes have been put forward for this reversal; the swing in medical opinion away from the value of medicinal waters; the new taste for Romanticism which took visitors to the wider beauties of the Lake District and Alps; the rise of evangelism, which heard denunciations of the very foundations of Bath's prosperity from the majority of the town's pulpits; political changes, which led to the election of a Radical – indistinguishable from a revolutionary to much of Bath's clientele – in the Reform election of 1832. ▓ Whatever the cause, belief in the reviving properties of the railway was commercially driven, given Bath's perennial reliance on an influx of visitors; logical, given its position throughout the centuries as the hub of a local and national network of communications; and talismanic, since it had been *Ralph Allen's* exploitation of *Padmore's* prototype railway which had enabled the transportation from *Combe Down* of the stone which had shaped the town. It was, however, mainly misplaced. The railway did not merely fail to deliver the expected visitors, it slowly but surely destroyed the old coaching and inn trades with which Bath had enjoyed a symbiotic relationship for centuries. To add insult to injury, excavation during construction of the line had revealed extensive reserves of high quality freestone a few miles to the east at *Box*, providing unwanted and powerful competition for the operations which survived within Bath. ▓ The town however retained some of the side effects of its previous glories, most notably on the service side of the economy (although for a town often considered to exist independently of industry its tally of forty-six exhibitors at the *Great Exhibition* of 1851 is surprisingly high) and was noted for its high class retailing, and for the medical and other professional services which would naturally have congregated around a wealthy, elderly, and not especially healthy clientele. Although much quieter now than its its heyday, and no longer the fashionable epicentre of England, Bath remained an exceptionally civilized residence for those able to afford it. ▓ In 1874 the railway finally appeared to make good

■ *BATH SPA HOTEL*
SYDNEY ROAD
Set among seven acres of land-scaped gardens within ten minutes' walk of the town centre, this handsome hotel was built in 1835 to recreate the classic elegance of Bath, and continues to provide service in the traditional English style

■ *THE THEATRE ROYAL*
Begun in 1804, a part of the
building was originally the home
of Beau Nash: also retained is a
bust of David Garrick, the noted
18th century actor

its promise of redemption when the conjunction of the Somerset and Dorset line with the Midland Railway, forming a north-south link, concluded a programme of civic redevelopment aimed at reinstating the spa as a social centre, with an 'Attractions Society' aggressively marketed Bath in the London, provincial, and overseas press. From the mid 1870s the large hotels accommodated an increasing stream of visitors, which became a flood in 1880 after the *Great Roman Bath* had been unearthed by the City Engineer, *Major Davis*, and exhibited to a fascinated public. 🔳 This completion of the historical circle provided a new impetus to civic ingenuity, which culminated in the *Bath Historical Pageant* of 1909. With its cast of pigs (representing *Bladud*'s contribution), Romans, Cavaliers, Roundheads, Georgians Victorians, heroes and villains, the pageant achieved international fame and was conceived both as a firm location of Bath in its past and as an expression of confidence in its future. Within five years such hopes had been set aside as Bath and England entered the twentieth century on the battlefields of northern Europe.

ESSENTIAL BATH

No book can ever hope to capture purely by repetition of historical fact the combination of fascinating past and vibrant present which makes Bath unique. Nor can physical description match the power of personal experience in appreciating Bath's particular beauties. ▦ *One can, however, focus on Bath's more important features, and gain from them some further insight into its remarkable and continuing story.*

The Abbey

BATH ABBEY is the fourth great religious foundation to occupy the same site at the centre of Bath. The first was the temple of *Minerva* in *Aquae Sulis*, the second the church which housed the coronation of *Edgar*, first *King of All England*. The third was the original abbey, created by *John of Tours*, which for a brief period in the early *Middle Ages* made Bath one of the most important centres of religious authority in England. According to legend the building which now stands before us was inspired by a dream in which angels ascended to heaven on ladders accompanied by a voice intoning 'Let an olive establish the crown and a king restore the church'. The dreamer, *Bishop Oliver King*, had little difficulty in understanding the commission and his central role in implementing the instruction, and construction was begun in 1499. The secret of Bath Abbey's particular beauty lies in its scale. It does not possess the massive grandeur of a York Minster or Nôtre Dame, which would overwhelm its surroundings, nor does it have the natural advantage of a spectacularly prominent setting enjoyed by the likes of Durham and Laôn. Perpendicular Gothic in essence, its ornate pinnacles and delicately flung buttresses give it a fragile, almost jewel-like appearance which conspires with its modest size to set it off in perfect counterpoint to the more robustly angular edifices which surround it. One particular detail stands out, the sculpted angels ascending ladders on the west front. Particularly expressive of a mediaeval perspective which would have been unthinkable to the architects who were later to shape Bath, one may have reservations as to whether the spiritual grace of the protaganists is perfectly represented by their monkey-like scrambling up the vertical wall. What is certain is that the façade demonstrates a literal approach to divine inspiration which is especially captivating in its naive vigour and charm. Unlike most English

cathedrals and abbeys, the interior presents an unimpeded view along its east-west axis, concluded at each end by the magnificent windows which have led it to be known as 'the lantern of England'. Equally noteworthy is the fan-vaulted roof, originally conceived by *Robert* and *William Vertue*, pioneering masters of the art, but only completed in stages over the course of the abbey's history. The last section of roof to be completed, that over the nave, was put in place during the second half of the last century.

Pulteney Bridge

IT IS PERHAPS surprising that the high priest of the *Palladian* ethic, **Robert Adam**, has only one work to represent him in the most overtly Palladian town in Europe. Its origins, as with so much of Bath's fabric, reside in the great surge of building wich took place between the years 1765 and 1775. ▨ *Pulteney Bridge* was originally conceived as the first stage in the establishment of a new estate, planned by a Scots landowner (and husband of the heiress *Frances Pulteney*) called *William Johnstone* to develop a new residential area on the hitherto unoccupied farmland on the other side of the *Avon* to Bath. Johnstone called upon Adam to design both the estate, to be called Bathwick, and the river crossing on which the success of the development depended. After examination of the plans the **Corporation of Bath** rejected Adam's designs for the estate on environmental grounds, expressing the fear that 'the smoke will greatly incommode the neighbourhood' – although it must also

■ *PULTENEY BRIDGE*
The elegant interior walkway lined with shops

be remembered that the Corporation saw little financial benefit, and significant reduction in their civic powers, in such speculative developments – and Johnstone's estate of **Bathwick** failed to translate from Adam's drawing board. ▨ However, despite modification and delay, his beautiful bridge was realised, and remains one of the masterpieces of Bath. Nor is there another bridge of its scale like it in England. On its exterior three deep arches form the solid foundation for a high walled symmetry of some severity, lightened by the effect of the weir which sparkles at its foot. Its interior is much lighter, the proportions more intimate, to create an elegant façade for the shops which line its walkway. ▨ For fifteen years the frustrations experienced by *William Johnstone Pulteney* (as he was now

known) meant that Pulteney Bridge led only to the watermill and the small cluster of buildings which then comprised Bathwick. Eventually lifehold tenancies on the important land expired with their owners, and today it continues into the more ostentatious boulevardism of **Great Pulteney Street**, impressively scaled at 100 feet wide and 1100 feet long. Designed by **Thomas Baldwin** under the guidance of Pulteney and intended as a the last word in desirable residential property, it quickly became one of the most fashionable addresses in Bath. Although one could present a strong case for the proportions being out of scale for a town of Bath's size, and bridle at its unrelenting uniformity of perspective, one cannot help be slightly awed despite such objections, as by any expression of overweening architectural confidence.

■ *GENERAL TRADING COMPANY, ARGYLE STREET*
Located in elegant Georgian premises, its three floors offer a wealth of stylish gifts and accessories for the home which combine with a relaxed ambience to provide an easy and enjoyable shopping experience

King's and Queen's Baths

THE THERMAL WATERS of Bath rose to the surface in three distinct spots, which became the sites of three distinct bathing establishments: the *Hot Bath*, the *Cross Bath*, and the most intensely developed of the three, the *King's Bath*. This utilised the same spring which the Romans had diverted and dammed for their *Great Bath*, and was begun in the twelfth century by *John of Tours*, who albeit unexplicitly named the complex the King's Bath after *Henry I*, the second of his royal patrons. It was during the reinstallation of the baths as a central facet of Bath life that the historian *Geoffrey of Monmouth*, citing an unnamed earlier source, first recorded the legend of *Bladud*. ▨ Throughout the middle ages the King's Bath was the principal focus of what might be termed the bathing economy, and the principal target of those objecting to its associated activities. In truth the relationship between the afflicted visitor and those tending to his or her needs was open to abuse. It is easy to see how mutually-beneficial arrangements might spring up between physicians, apothecaries, and the lodging-houses which at one time surrounded the baths, and equally easy to see how these might not be to the ultimate benefit of their clientele, the patients seeking a cure. It is probably to the town's advantage that, as the baths became increasingly resorts of the fashionable, so the need to provide a cure for the seriously ill diminished. However, despite abuses the Corporation made significant efforts to regularise proceedings, and certainly the baths were not the scene of constant riot and disorder they are so often portrayed as. Mixed nude bathing scandalised some, though doubtless delighted others, and numerous attempts to outlaw the practice were attempted between 1621 to 1625, but in many other ways the Corporation made great strides in making Bath as welcoming as possible to visitors. Like the Romans the Corporation

■ *KING'S AND QUEEN'S BATHS*
The Queen's Bath enjoyed cooler water than the King's Bath, and was constructed, originally for feminine use only, several centuries after its neighbour

appointed attendants to assist bathers and ensure proper order, and rules were laid down for the refilling of the baths and for the supply of cold water for the public drinking fountains. Such measures, as well as the continuance of the propaganda begun by Geoffrey of Monmouth and maintained by medical writers in the early seventeenth century, ensured that Bath more than held its own in competition with Buxton and Tunbridge Wells for wealthy patrons. ▓ The Queen's Bath was so named in honour of *Anne of Denmark*, wife of *James I*, who bathed in it in 1616. Built in 1576 adjoining the King's Bath to accommodate the increasing numbers of bathers seeking a cure, it was removed during the excavation of the Roman baths in the late eighteenth century.

■ *BATH STREET*
Designed by Thomas Baldwin and built in the early 1790s, its delightful colonnades provided a protected passage from King's Bath to Cross Bath

Hot Bath & Cross Bath

THE TWO OTHER SOURCES of the hot springs within the walls of Bath, the *Hot* and *Cross Baths* were both originally developed by *Bishop Robert of Lewes* during the years of his rule from 1136 to 1166. Initially the two smaller baths seem to have acquired a more directly medicinal reputation than was claimed for the fashionable *King's Bath*. *John Leland*, who visited Bath at the time of the *Dissolution*, wrote that the Cross Bath is 'much frequented of people diseased with lepre, pokkes, scabbes and great aches', in comparison with the King's Bath: 'very faire and large… to this bathe do Gentilmen resort'. The Hot Bath was the preserve of serious bathers only, as the flow of the water from its underground caverns was so direct, and so diminished therefore was the time for cooling, that he declared it 'would scauld the flesch'. Cross Bath became a much more socially acceptable venue in the seventeenth century – Hot Bath remained too austere for any but the most ascetic sufferer. To set the seal on the reconciliation of Bath with the restored monarchy after the *Civil War*, Bath having after some soul-searching settled on the Parliamentary side on the outbreak of hostilities, *King Charles II* and his wife took the waters of Cross Bath in 1663, and this royal seal of approval was to bring about a permanent place for Bath in the constitution of England. Caught up in the question of the succession to Charles II, the Corporation of Bath had originally decided in favour of the *Duke of Monmouth*, but later in fear of losing their corporate privileges transferred their allegiance to his more powerful, but Catholic, brother *James*. Having assisted in James' accession, the town was then the cause of his downfall, when in 1687 James brought his hitherto barren queen, *Catherine of Braganza*, to bathe in Cross Bath in hope of an

■ *KINGSMEAD SQUARE*
Formerly a meadow outside the city walls favoured for duelling, it was here that Sheridan fought with a rival over the affections of Elizabeth Linley

■ *Hot Bath (With Cross Bath in the background)*
The failure of immersion in Cross Bath to provide an heir for the
wife of Charles II led to the rejection of a proposal to rename the bath
'Queen Caroline's Bath'

heir. Alas for James the waters succeeded – no doubt with some assistance – and the sudden reality of the perpetuation of a Catholic dynasty was sufficient to prompt the **Glorious Revolution**, the invitation to **William of Orange** to reinstate the Protestant monarchy, and the limitation of royal power in perpetuity. To the efficacy of the waters of Cross Bath can be ascribed the fact that no English prince can marry a Catholic bride if he wishes one day to ascend the throne.

■ *Stakis Bath, Widcombe Basin (Thimble Mill pictured)*
Enjoying matchless views from its conservatory restaurant over the confluence of the Kennet & Avon canal and the river Avon, this friendly and efficient hotel offers stylish facilities within two minutes walk of the city centre

The Commercial Artery

ROM ITS CONCEPTION, *Milson Street* has occupied a central position in the life of Bath which has been maintained throughout the last two hundred years. Named after *Daniel Milsom*, a wine cooper turned property developer, construction was begun in 1762 to form a link between the old social centre of the lower town and the newly-fashionable upper town which was emerging at that time. Running in a broad downhill sweep from *George Street* to *Upper Borough Walls*, the thoroughfare rapidly attracted business away from the traditional commercial areas, and by 1795 was firmly established both as the principal artery linking the lower and upper towns and as a fashionable centre in its

own right – although it was in Milsom Street that *Sir Walter Elliott* in *Persuasion* 'counted eighty-seven women go by, without there being a tolerable face among them'. ▨ The east side of the upper part of the street is dominated by *Thomas Baldwin*'s *Somersetshire Buildings*, with their confident façade facing across the street to where *James Jolly* established in 1831 the

■ *No. 5 Trim Street*
Home of General Wolfe, hero of the Heights of Abraham, which crucial battle is reported to have lasted no more than eleven minutes

emporium selling linen, silk, china, and knick-knacks which still bears his name. Now dedicated to a much wider ranger of consumer goods, *Jolly's* has carefully preserved both its exterior and the standard of service for which Bath is rightly famed, and James Jolly's imposing façade continues to dominate the west side of the street. Further down on the east side stands the Octogon, built in 1767 as a chapel which rapidly achieved such fashionable status that, as *Mrs Piozzi* reports on visiting it to hear the *Bishop of Gloucester* preach, the congregation was packed in 'like seeds in a sunflower'. The building

now serves as an exhibition room for the **Royal Photographic Society**, an optical legacy all the more appropriate since in 1781 the chapel's organist, the astronomer **William Herschel**, designed and produced the telescope which enabled him on 13 March 1781 to reveal for the first time to a meeting of the **Bath Philosophical Society** the existence of the planet **Uranus**. Milsom Street encapsulates the attraction of Bath in a single thoroughfare – a gracious and elegant historical setting for all the amenities of modern life.

■ *JOLLY'S*

Jolly's is probably the oldest department store in the world. A £2.5m refurbishment, to recreate the character and excitement of the original emporium, will be completed in September 1995

Queen's Square

■ *QUEEN'S PARADE PLACE*
The location of the only remaining examples of sedan chair houses in Britain. Until regulated by Nash, Bath's sedan chair carriers were reputedly the most offensive hirelings in Europe

■ *FRANCIS HOTEL,*
QUEEN'S SQUARE
Occupying a row of the former houses which comprise Queen's Square, the interior complements its elegant exterior. Rooms facing onto the square gardens are among the most eagerly sought after in Bath

UEEN'S SQUARE was the first of *John Wood the Elder*'s great masterpieces to reach fruition and, as has already been outlined (Seizing the Day), was the prototype for the method of the develop spreading risk by subletting plots to individual builders which enabled the transformation of Bath into the city we see today. Conceived to take advantage of the growing numbers of fashionable visitors wishing to make an extended stay in Bath, the success of the project played a major part in ensuring that the demand for property in the town would increase to a hitherto unimagined extent. ▨ The development was built entirely for private residences, but to an integrated plan and with an extraordinary overall grandeur in comparison to the comparatively modest proportions of the individual dwellings. The most flamboyant of the four sides of the square is the showpiece north front, with seven houses, one of which Wood retained for his own use, forming a palatial façade which successfully avoids any semblance of domesticity. The remaining three sides do not suffer unduly by comparison, and the whole must have appeared even more imposing as it grew up over the ten years after 1729 out of what had previously been meadows. ▨ In order to imagine Queen's Square as it first appeared, and as Wood intended, it is necessary not only to wish away the traffic but also to dispense with the trees now growing in the central area, which had been carefully designed as an open space with gravel walks and tended lawns in which the residents might assemble and promenade. The uninterrupted view across the quadrangle also provided a suitable setting for the obelisk erected by *Beau Nash* in 1738 'in memory of honours conferr'd and in gratitude for benefits bestowed in this city by his royal highness *Frederick, Prince of Wales*'.

The somewhat ludicrous figure of Frederick was thus accorded greater honour by Nash than he was allowed by his parents *George II* and *Caroline* (his mother, after whom the square was named), who once observed that 'My dear first born is the greatest ass and the greatest liar… and the greatest beast in the whole world, and I heartily wish he were out of it'. The author of this sweeping parental curse must have been even more dismayed by the manner of his swift acquiescence with her wishes, when he became probably the only heir apparent in history to be denied his destiny by the fatal impact of a tennis ball. The obelisk in his memory still stands, although it was renovated in 1978 to celebrate both the 25th anniversary of the coronation of *Elizabeth II* and the 250th anniversary of Wood's design.

■ *QUEEN'S SQUARE*
Now laid with grass and informal gardens, Wood's original design envisaged a flat open space giving uninterrupted views of the whole development

The Royal Crescent

■ *THE ROYAL VICTORIA PARK*
One of the earliest public parks in
Britain, it features an obelisk
chronicling the progress of Victoria
from accession to death, and offers
excellent views of the Royal Crescent

THE IDEA FOR the *Royal Crescent* was conceived by *John Wood the elder* and completed after the death of his father in 1754 by the younger Wood in the years 1767 to 1775. It is therefore yet another product of that most extraordinarily fertile decade of Bath's history, and it is equally astonishing to record that it represents the first time that a crescent of houses had been used in Britain. ▨ In simple terms the crescent is merely an extension of the principle of his father's previous developments, whereby a grandiose edifice is created by adjoining a row of separate houses within a single unifying plan, but the contrast with the earlier works is immediate. Where *Queen's Square* and *The Circus* formed enclosed spaces, this, possibly the finest crescent in Europe, was laid out to look over and embrace open landscape, its sweeping lawn becoming a favoured promenade for more than two centuries of visitors, with the drama of its impact enhanced by its approach through what was originally the only possible access along Brock Street. ▨ It is possible that this more exocentric aspect merely relects a change in architectural tastes, with a growing tendency towards the 'picturesque', the appreciation of unspoilt nature, making use of the natural curves of the terrain and looking across the valley of the Avon to the green hills opposite. One accidental explanation for this invention of a whole new architectural approach is that, owing to a temporary shortage of investment capital, construction of two of the three sections of The Circus was put on hold for a period of seven years: perhaps the arc of the single standing segment inspired the crescent form. A more esoteric conception, somehow more in keeping with the visionary impulses which we know inspired much of Wood the elder's architectural vision (and therefore all the more credible) is that Wood was convinced – although no-one seems to know whence

came the idea — that a crescent-shaped druidical temple dedicated to the moon once stood near **Stonehenge**. Possibly Wood the younger shared this belief, or merely humoured this conceit of his father's restless mind. ▦ So strong is the line of the terrace, so well integrated into its environment, that the magnificent sickle-shaped row of houses requires little else by way of decoration than the series of giant Ionic columns which punctuate and divide its length. Whatever the process of its conception, the resulting crescent is surely one of the world's finest urban landscapes.

■ *The Priory Hotel,*
Weston Road
Over the years the Priory Hotel and
Restaurant has gained international
acclaim for the excellence of its food
and fine wines, while its peaceful
location and superb gardens ensure
a memorable experience for residents
and non-residents alike

The Circus

IN MANY WAYS The Circus is the most perfect expression of *John Wood the elder's* extraordinary vision, enshrining as it does the quasi-mystical elements of his inspiration. The author of books on the significance of the megalithic temples at *Stonehenge* and *Stanton Drew*, he maintained that each of the seven hills of Bath was once dedicated to a single heavenly body whose worship was directed from a temple of *Apollo* in the centre of the town, and was a fervent believer in the story of *Bladud's* founding of Bath. And as we also know, Wood was a true Palladian admirer of the classical tradition, and was particularly proud of his home town's special links with Rome, to the extent that he had originally proposed the recreation of Bath based on the model of ancient *Rome* with a forum, circus, and gymnasium. Thus two antithetical models, the *Colosseum* of classical Rome — contemporaries rather disparagingly referred to The Circus as 'the Colosseum turned inside out', as if this was an everyday achievement — and the druidic temple of Stonehenge — the diameter of which it echoed, albeit according to Wood's idiosyncratic personal system of measurement — were synthesised to produce a development which carries echoes of both, but which in its turn became a completely new type of edifice.

To someone intrigued by the conspiracy between architecture and mysticism, and the way in which buildings are sometimes used as spiritual riddles, The Circus is a fascinating subject. It provides a continual restatement of trinities: the three great crescents of the Circus, intersticed with their three exit roads, featured columns of all three *Greek* orders of architecture. The parapets were adorned with acorns in reference both to the Bladud myth and to the druids, establishing with the Greek and Roman elements a confluence of three traditions of antiquity into which Wood wished to re-establish

■ *THE QUEENSBERRY HOTEL, RUSSELL STREET*
A luxury town house hotel set in the heart of Georgian Bath. Under the direction of Stephen and Penny Ross it has also won wide fame for its award-winning Olive Tree Restaurant

his home town, while many symbols associated with freemasonry are displayed in the carvings at the first level. The true believer will find many further elements on which to build pyramids of convergence. ▨ The first crescent was rapidly completed, but an untimely drying up of credit delayed the completion of the project until 1766. By this time the visionary whose extraordinary designs had done so much to assist the creation of a new town had been dead twelve years, leaving his son John to oversee the final realisation of his most cherished dream.

■ *THE CIRCUS: DETAIL*
Almost without repetition, the emblems depicted on the frieze at the first level are rife with arcane and esoteric significance

Walcot

THE VICINITY OF THE first crossing of the *Avon*, and a nodal point therefore of the primeval *Jurassic Way* and of the *Roman Fosse Way* which supplanted it, the area we now know as *Walcot* was the original heart of what is now Bath. Best indications suggest that it was the site of the garrison established by the Romans to protect the river crossing, their primary military objective in the region. As the focus of the town moved south to surround the hot springs, Walcot found itself outside the town walls, although it maintained its status as the market centre of the area. The tide of residence and enterprise has ebbed and flowed along the *London Road* for centuries, but it was only with the *Georgian* boom that Walcot was transformed from a poor hamlet on the outskirts of Bath to one of the most valuable development sites in the country.

Constructed on *The Paragon* at the apex of this development, the *Countess of Huntingdon's Chapel* is one of Bath's most facinating buildings. It was erected at the behest of *Selina Shirley, Countess of Huntingdon*, one of the sixty-plus children produced by *Earl Ferrers* with the assistance of two wives and sundry others. Perhaps unsurprisingly, his daughter was renowned for her virtue and the strength of her religious beliefs, which found their true home in the Methodist faith in purity of thought and simple rigour of doctrine. The Countess devoted her life and considerable wealth to the Methodist movement, and chose to build the fourth of the chapels she financed in a town which she had grown to know through frequent health visits, and which was a byword for the laxness of its lifestyle and its widespread indulgence of vice. So impressed was *John Wesley* by what he saw that he averred that preaching in Bath was like 'attacking the Devil in his own

headquarters' (in turn, *Horace Walpole* observed that Wesley was 'as obviously

an actor as Garrick'). Opening on 6 October 1765, what is most apparent

about the Chapel is its antipathy to its surroundings. Unlike almost every

other building of that classic age dedicated to the pursuit of comfortable

living according to external ostentation of decorum and quiet taste, the

chapel aggressively thrusts its gothic parapeted façade at the moral laxity

which once sought to swamp it. Today the chapel houses the *Building of*

Bath Museum, which offers a comprehensive and entertaining insight into

how Bath took the shape in which we see it today.

■ *COUNTESS OF*
HUNTINGDON'S CHAPEL
Established as a bulwark against
the moral laxity perceived to be
swamping Bath, the last religious
service was held in 1981

Lansdown

■ *Somerset Place*
With the emphatic broken
pediment which forms its
dramatic centrepiece

THE DEVELOPMENT of the slopes to the north of the town was a further response to the opportunity for profit offered to developers by the continual demand for residential property throughout the latter half of the eighteenth century. The shape this development took was a response to the lead and example of Wood père et fils in the *Royal Crescent*. The viability and acceptability of the crescent for a line of residences having been established, this form was developed by allowing it a less formal, more sinuous, line as it followed the natural contours of its location. This extension of the taste for the picturesque first recognised in the Royal Crescent was given full rein in *John Palmer*'s *Lansdown Crescent*, completed in around 1780, with its serpentine route across the upper slopes looking down over green grass still kept under control by the occasional introduction of sheep. ▦ Architecturally Lansdown Crescent is less striking, with refined pilasters rather than the almost disproportionately bold columns of Wood's original, but the same certainly cannot be said of *Somerset Place* which continues its path to the west. This was the brainchild of *John Eveleigh*, in which the central detail of a pair of houses surmounted by a broken pediment crowned with an urn stands in noble contrast with the almost austere decorum of the façade of the crescent. Building of Somerset Place was begun in 1789, but was halted in its tracks by the outbreak of war with revolutionary France in 1793. ▦ The battle for supremacy in Europe had been an ongoing thorn in Bath's side throughout the century: in 1764, two years after the agreement of a contested peace, lodging-house keepers, one of the principal markers of prices in the town, had given the interruption of supplies of essential items as the cause of being forced to extend high season prices to nine months of the year, and the following year soaring

food prices raised the spectre of hunger riots. However, the crash of 1793 was altogether more spectacular. With financial credit already stretched by speculative mania, the prospect of a long war with an old enemy in a new and sinister guise caused the collapse of two of Bath's five banks; the chain of risk-spreading pioneered by Wood was rudely sundered by a string of interrelated bankruptcies and construction work all over the city ground to a halt. In the case of Somerset Place the development was not completed until thirty years after work had begun.

■ *LANSDOWN CRESCENT*
The relative lack of adornment on the façade serves to emphasise the natural grace of its sinuous path along the contour

Prior Park

THE STORY of *Ralph Allen* is an archetype of Bath at its most vigorous. Arguably the most remarkable of the triumvirate – Ralph Allen, *Beau Nash*, and *John Wood the elder* – responsible for the town's development in its most fertile period of the eighteenth century, Allen arrived in Bath from Cornwall as assistant postmaster in 1710 and within two years had become the youngest postmaster in the country. Within fifteen years he had amassed sufficient wealth to enable him to buy the stone quarries at *Combe Down*

and commission an ingenious prototypical railway designed by *John Padmore* to carry huge blocks of stone, the raw materials for Wood's West Country renaissance, to Bath. This venture in turn provided him with yet another personal fortune, enabling him to commission Wood to design and build *Prior Park*: in the slightly barbed words of *Philip Thicknesse*, 'a noble seat which sees all Bath, and which was built… for all Bath to see'. His principal residence of Prior Park makes use of a delightful confluence of location and prospect. Previously the holding of the priors of Bath, the land offered Wood an opportunity to demonstrate his equal respect both for the Palladian tradition and for those dark northern spirits of wood sky and water which stimulated his fertile brain. For example, the north front demonstrates Palladianism at full pitch and volume, with its great portico of Corinthian columns, yet is in such perfect scale with its surroundings that what would elsewhere seem bombastic here seems merely appropriate. A further perfectly picturesque touch is the bridge over the fishponds, based on that at *Wilton House*, which provides a sublime example of the correct juxtaposition of formal architecture with a romantic context.

The initial source of Allen's wealth is still disputed. It is generally held that, by opening what were intended as sealed and therefore confidential mails, he was able to uncover and expose a Jacobite plot to *General Wade*. Whether true or not, what is certain is that under the patronage of the good general he completely reorganised the national postal system, instituting a system of 'cross posts' which proved far more efficient than the inadequate and costly system which had hitherto prevailed. What is certain is that Allen used his wealth both wisely and with good intent, contributing generously to many good causes. Even so acute a judge of human frailty as *Fielding* gave him a glowing reference: 'hospitable to his neighbours, charitable to the poor, and benevolent to all mankind'.

■ *HOMEWOOD PARK,* (*INSET*) *HINTON CHARTERHOUSE Standing in ten acres overlooking a designated area of outstanding natural beauty, Homewood Park Hotel and Restaurant offers both informal luxury and a nationally-renowned restaurant*

Bath Today

BATH IS A UNIQUE architectural phenomenon, a beautiful and seemingly harmonious whole that was the happy consequence as much of human self interest and greed as of any overriding plan or intention to produce an end result which is one of the finest achievements of Western civilization. ▨ One factor however has remained constant throughout Bath's extraordinary past. Since the days of the *Romans*, Bath it has depended for its success on satisfying the needs of its visitors. Throughout the centuries it has been required to provide its guests with the services they require, from the provision of healing waters, to medical attention, to the highest quality retail goods. With due respect to those industries such as *Stothert & Pitt* which have maintained a presence in the town over many years, the economic well-being of the town depends as it has always done on the continuation of the vast numbers of visitors who now throng to its world-renowned sights. And just as a visitor to *Venice* may find it hard to envisage that there are people who reside in that dreamlike city and who go about their daily round as window cleaners or mechanics, so it is sometimes hard to imagine Bath as anything other than a town which exists as a historic site for our delectation. But Bath is not a theme park: it is a town subject like any other to the pressures of modern life. ▨ Not the least of these pressures is environmental. At first oblivious of the treasures in its charge, when hundreds of Georgian cottages were demolished to make way for unsightly modern housing devoid of social facilities, the Corporation in the early part of this century rapidly became aware of its responsibilities. *The Bath Act* of 1925 gave it new powers in the city, including the regulation of building styles and materials

■ *LUCKNAM PARK*

An exquisite country house, just six miles from the Bath, with 42 individually decorated bedrooms and one Michelin star for the highly regarded restaurant. It has its own Equestrian Centre and extensive Leisure Spa.

and the control of traffic. 1932 saw the creation of a *Planning Area of Bath*, in an attempt to prevent the city's green fringes from being overwhelmed by excessive development – ironic, given that it was precisely the mania for development which created that which was now in need of preservation: had the Corporation had similar powers when the mediaeval town was destroyed to make way for new development, much of what we now cherish might not exist. In 1937 a new *Bath Act* further increased the powers of the Corporation, enabling the listing for preservation of important buildings predating 1820. During the *Second World War* the *'Baedecker Raids'* (in retaliation for the Allied bombing of Rostock and Lübeck) saw serious damage

■ *THE MODERN CITY*
Visitors and residents mingle in
Bath's beatifully preserved
thoroughfares

to more than a thousand buildings. By 1945 traffic congestion and atmospheric pollution had become sufficiently serious to warrant scientific analysis: in ten thousand years we will see the effects apparent in the waters of the springs. It is to the eternal credit of the Corporation that their efforts to preserve the town were recognised in 1988 by the addition of Bath to the *UNESCO World Heritage List* as a site of global importance. ▨ The war also saw the curtailment of bathing and taking water, as the major hotels were turned over to the admiralty for the duration. This drying up of health visitors was another crucial episode in Bath's history. Never again would the healing waters be the focus of attraction, and since that time the emphasis has returned to another mainstay of its economy. For centuries retailing had been a necessary ancillary to the main businesses of bathing, gambling, and taking water: it now became an attraction in its own right, and today Bath's shops fulfil the role both of a regional shopping centre and a support to national and international tourism. Other attractions have emerged to provide invigorating injections into both the financial and emotional well-being of the town, from the annual *Bath Festival* which was inaugurated in 1948 to the hot air ballooning which regularly enlivens Bath's magnificent skyscapes. Hotels and restaurants of the highest quality, in a concentration unmatched in a town of comparable size, cater to the physical needs of visitors. Perhaps better than any other town in the world, Bath has succeeded in harmonising the glories of the past and the comforts of the present.

■ *STON EASTON PARK,*
STON EASTON
Placed amidst oaks in gardens sloping gently to the river Norr which were landscaped by Humphry Repton in 1793, Ston Easton Park combines all the warmth of a family home with a beautifully preserved eighteenth century Palladian mansion. Even the kitchens and wine cellars retain their original appearance

■ *PAXTON & WHITFIELD,*
1 JOHN STREET
Situated between Milsom Street and Queen's Square, the country's oldest-established cheesemonger has been supplying a wide range of high quality British and international merchandise since the days of the Napoleonic war

Distributors of Past and Present

Apsley House
141 Newbridge Hill
Bath, Avon BA1 3PT
Tel: (01225) 336 966
Fax: (01225) 425 462

Bath Spa Hotel
Sydney Road
Bath, Avon BA2 6JF
Tel: (01225) 444 424
Fax: (01225) 444 006

Combe Grove Manor
Brassknocker Hill
Monkton, Combe
Nr Bath, Avon BA2 7HS
Tel: (01225) 834 644
Fax: (01225) 834 961

Francis Hotel
Queen Square
Bath, Avon BA1 2HH
Tel: (01225) 424 257
Fax: (01225) 319 715

General Trading Company
10 Argyle Street
Pulteney Bridge
Bath, Avon BA2 4BQ
Tel: (01225) 460 907
Fax: (01225) 448 596

Hilton National
Walcot Street
Bath, Avon BA1 5BJ
Tel: (01225) 463 411
Fax: (01225) 464 393

Homewood Park
Hinton Charterhouse
Bath, Avon BA3 6BB
Tel: (01225) 723 731
Fax: (01225) 723 820

Hunstrete House
Hunstrete, Chelwood
Nr Bath, Avon BS18 4NS
Tel: (01761) 490 490
Fax: (01761) 490 732

Jolly's
House of Fraser
(Stores) Limited
Milsom Street
Bath, Avon BA1 1DD
Tel: (01225) 462 811
Fax: (01225) 443 274

Lucknam Park
Colerne
Wiltshire SN14 8AZ
Tel: (01225) 742 777
Fax: (01225) 743 536

Paxton & Whitfield
1 John Street
Bath, Avon BA1 2JL
Tel: (01225) 466 403

Priory Hotel
Weston Road
Bath, Avon BA1 2XT
Tel: (01225) 331 922
Fax: (01225) 448 276

Queensberry Hotel
Russell Street
Bath, Avon BA1 2QF
Tel: (01225) 447 928
Fax: (01225) 446 065

Stakis Bath
Widcombe Basin
Bath, Avon BA2 4JP
Tel: (01225) 338 855
Fax: (01225) 428 941

Ston Easton Park
Ston Easton
Nr Bath, Avon BA3 4DF
Tel: (01761) 241 631
Fax: (01761) 241 377

Authors' Note

Although a number of sources were used in preparing the text, we are particularly indebted to Trevor Fawcett and Stephen Bird's "Bath History and Guide" (Alan Sutton Publishing) recommended for anyone seeking greater detail on Bath's history.

Past & Present Publications
Ptarmigan House
No 9 The Coda Centre
189 Munster Road
London SW6 6AW
Telephone: 0171-381 5600
Facsimile: 0171-381 4012